Pandemic Press Media Magazine

Summer 2022 Volume 1, Issue 1

I0176066

Inside This Issue:

Letter From The Editors

Hello! And welcome to our debut edition of Pandemic Press Media Magazine! We are very honored and humbled to make this next project a reality!

This magazine is a mix of all of our projects; including some things that are revealed for the first time! Our hope is that you enjoy this publication!

Thank you for all of your continued love and support that you show us each and every day! Thank you once again! God Bless!

Cover Story

One on one with Summarae!!

We were blessed to have Musical Artist Summarae stop by PPM Magazine for a one on one interview!

PPM Magazine: Summarae, thank you so much for stopping by for this interview!

SR: Thank you for having me!

PPM Magazine: How did you come up with the concepts of your songs?

Interview continued on this next page...

SR: Well, most of my songs are inspired by an event or another person. "Love Hurts," that was my very first single. That was inspired by a disagreement that I had with my husband. And of course I embellished a little bit. (HAHA!) But, that's where the inspiration for "Love Hurts" came from. "You Are" was inspired by a friend of mine who was in a new relationship. "Come with Me" was inspired by "Hail Mary" by Tupac. He was one of my favorite artists.

PPM Magazine: Of all the songs that you've made so far, do you have a favorite one?

SR: Well, I don't think that I have a favorite; because they are all unique. Kind of like your children. They are all unique in their own special way.

PPM Magazine: Speaking of your music Summarae, how does music get from here in America to overseas?

SR: Some of the music is shared. " Love Hurts" was played by Kid Capri. He played "Love Hurts" as well as quite a few DJs. DJ Niceness, from the UK was the first one to play it. You know, it's up to the radio stations and the DJs to get the world out. Plus, I've been networking with folks from other countries.

PPM Magazine: Can you elaborate on the difference between being an Indie artist vs. other artists?

SR: As far as being an Indie artist, I find one thing interesting, hip hop and a lot of mainstream R&B uses a lot of samples. As an Independent artist, you hear "That sounds like such and such. Be original." Another thing is that you don't have the resources. The music is free. It takes thousands and thousands of dollars to make one song. But, you can get it for free. You can stream it and that's that!

PPM Magazine: We enjoy streaming and listening to all of your songs. Have you ever considered doing a Christmas album?

SR: You may be the third person to ask me that. I haven't really considered it. I don't know if you know this but I used to perform in a couple of bands in Pittsburgh. Shoutout to House of Soul and Top Flight Band. Top Flight Band I sang with for maybe 5 years. House of Soul I sang with for 1 year. And then, I kind of moved away from cover songs.

PPM Magazine: Summarae, it's an honor to have had you speak with us!

SR: Thank you! I always have so much fun with you two! It's just an honor to be here!

PPM Magazine: If someone wanted to reach out or connect with you, how would they do so?

SR: I'm on all social media. You can find me at S-U-M-M-A-R-A-E. That's Facebook, Twitter, Instagram, under my name. I'm also on Youtube and Spotify. Hit me up and send me a message. I'll reply!

PPM Magazine: Well, Summarae, thank you for finding time to speak with us! We would love to have you come back in the future!

SR: I'd love to! Thank you so much for having me!

Cooking Fun with Mrs. Cubbage!!

Helloooooo, Everybody!! I'm so happy to have you here! I'm Mrs. Cubbage! I am an author, early childhood educator, wife, daughter, sister, friend, podcaster, certified life coach and entrepreneur! One thing I love doing is teaching! Teaching people. Especially young people. One thing that I really enjoy is teaching young people how to cook. Once they master that skill; along with gaining the confidence to excel in the kitchen, everything else that they try to do is easy! New episodes of my show are available Fridays at 4PM EST on The CCI Radio Show YouTube Channel!

Here are a few recipes from my book, "Cooking Fun with Mrs. Cubbage" that you and your family are sure to LOVE!

Fresh Garden Salad

Ingredients:
1 Head of Lettuce
3 Tomatoes
2 Carrots
3 Cucumbers
Your child's favorite salad dressing

Directions:
Make sure to wash all vegetables before use.
On a cutting board, cut all of the vegetables into small bite sized pieces, adding to a large salad bowl.
Add the salad dressing. And serve!

Fresh Chicken Salad

For this recipe, you need to look at the "Fresh garden salad" recipe, then add chicken breast! That's all! Very yummy! And VERY simple! Your child will enjoy this one...largely because of the chicken! HAHA!

Refer to the "Fresh garden salad" recipe on the previous page.

How to prepare the chicken.

- Heat ¼ tablespoon of oil or canola oil in a large skillet.

- Season the chicken breasts on both sides with salt, ground pepper, garlic powder and dried basil. When oil is hot, add chicken breasts to the pan – cook two chicken breasts at a time because you don't want to overcrowd your skillet.

- Cook chicken breasts for 7 to 10 minutes. Flip the chicken breasts over, add a tablespoon of butter to the skillet, and continue to cook for 7 more minutes, or until internal temperature reaches 165F. Cooking time will always depend on the thickness of the chicken breasts. When finished, transfer chicken breasts to a cutting board; let rest for 5 minutes, then slice and add to the salad and serve

Check out more great recipes with Mrs. Cubbage on our YouTube Channel, **The**

CCI Radio Show!

The Music Spotlight w/ Sam C. Smooth

Welcome to the debut and this edition of The Music Spotlight with Sam C. Smooth! I will give you the latest music news along with my own "Top 10" Albums and Singles of the summer from my favorite music genres. Let's get started!

Latest music news:

Per Billboard, recent singles released by musical artists Kendrick Lamar and Morgan Wallen debuted into the Top 10! Lamar debuted 4 songs, led by "N95" which reached #3. Wallen's "You Proof" reached #6. Congrats to both of these talented artists! And now, here are my picks for favorite singles and albums per genre for this edition of our magazine!

Sam C's 'Top 10' 80s Albums

1. Michael Jackson-Thriller

2. Purple Rain-Prince and the Revolution

3. Whitney Houston-Whitney Houston

4. Private Eyes-Hall And Oates

5. It Takes A Million Of Nations To Hold Us Back-Public Enemy

6. Madonna-Madonna

7. Rio-Duran Duran

8. Rapture-Anita Baker

9. 3 Feet High and Rising-De La Soul

10. Faith-George Michael

Sam C's 'Top 10' 80s Singles

1. Every Breath You Take-The Police

2. Eye Of The Tiger-Survivor

3. I Want To Know What Love Is-Foreigner

4. So Emotional-Whitney Houston

5. Sexual Healing-Marvin Gaye

6. Take On Me- A-Ha

7. The Sweetest Taboo-Sade

8. I Need Love-LL Cool J

9 . Somebody For Me-Heavy D And The Boyz

10. Sledgehammer-Peter Gabriel

Sam C's Top 10 Gospel Albums

1. The Best of Fred Hammond-Fred Hammond
2. God Period-E. Dewey Smith
3. Long Live Love-Kirk Franklin
4. Tribl 1-Tribl
5. Circles-Dante Bowe
6. Chosen Vessel-Marvin Sapp
7. The Best of the Staple Singers-Staple Singers
8. Heart, Passion, Pursuit-Tasha Cobbs Leonard
9. The Hill-Travis Greene
10. Best Days-Tamela Mann

Sam C's 'Top 10' Gospel Singles

1. I Can't Give Up-Byron Cage
2. Anyhow-Tye Tribett
3. In Jesus Name-Bebe Winans
4. Strong God-Kirk Franklin
5. Thank You For It All-Marvin Sapp
6. Stand Up-Damon Little
7. In Spite of Me-Tasha Cobbs Leonard
8. Never Lost- Cece Winans
9. Good & Loved-Travis Greene
10. Lifted Up-Vashawn Mitchell

Sam's 'Top 10' Smooth Jazz Albums

1. Heart To Heart-Norman Brown

2. All About Love-Norman Saunders

3. No Turning Back-Lowell Hopper

4. Tranquility- Les Sabler

5. Sunshine Radio-Tommy Guerrero

6. Let's Ride-The Smooth Jazz Alley

7. Lindsey Webster-I Didn't Mean It

8. Bridges-Cal Harris, Jr

9. A New Day-Dave Koz

10. Castella-Let Me Love You

Sam's 'Top 10' Smooth Jazz Singles

1. Breezin'-George Benson

2. Songbird-Kenny G

3. Sunday Strut-Blake Aaron

4. Coast to Coast-Pamela Williams

5. Maybe You Think-Vincent Ingala

6. Let's Go-Brian Culbertson

7. Dr. Norm-Dave Koz

8. Welcome to the Beach-Paul Hardcastle

9. Whatever She Wants-Chris Standring

10. Out to Lunch-Oli Silk

Sam C's 'Top 10' 90's Albums

1. One In A Million-Aaliyiah

2. The Chronic-Dr. Dre

3. Step Into The Arena-Gangstarr

4. Cracked Rear View-Hootie And The Blowfish

5. Jagged Little Pill-Alanis Morissette

6. Supernatural-Santana

7. The Velvet Rope-Janet Jackson

8. For The Cool In You-Babyface

9. Poison- Bell Biv Devoe

10. Funky Divas- En Vogue

Sam C's 'Top 10' 90s Singles

1. Killing Me Softly-The Fugees

2. Jam-Michael Jackson

3. I Want It That Way-Backstreet Boys

4. I Will Always Love You-Whitney Houston

5. No Scrubs- TLC

6. How Many Ways-Toni Braxton

7. Around The Way Girl- LL Cool J

8. Me And You- Toni Tony Tone

9. The Boy Is Mine- Brandy And Monica

10. The Mission-Special Ed

Sam C's 'Top 10' 70s Albums

1. Songs In The Key Of Life- Stevie Wonder

2. What's Going On-Marvin Gaye

3. The Payback-James Brown

4. Let's Stay Together-Al Green

5. Off The Wall- Michael Jackson

6. Silk Degrees- Boz Scaggs

7. Nightbirds-Labelle

8. Backstabbers- The O'Jays

9.Just As I Am- Bill Withers

10. The Heat Is On- The Isley Brothers

Sam C's 'Top 10' 70s Singles

1.Three Times A Lady- The Commodores

2. I'll Be There- The Jackson 5

3. Boogie Nights- Heatwave

4. Ring My Bell- Anita Ward

5. Love You Inside Out- The Bee Gees

6. Keep On Truckin'- Eddie Kendricks

7. Le Freak- Chic

8. Hot Stuff- Donna Summer

9. I Will Survive- Gloria Gaynor

10. Let's Get It On- Marvin Gaye

TLC Advice Column

Welcome to our ADVICE COLUMN. This is a place where letters from the public will be shared; no names will be used. And we will answer the letters to the best of our ability. Here is a copy of the first letter:

Dear TLC coaches,

I have a dilemma. I am a 35 year old woman who has been taught to be kind ,helpful and caring. But, as I grow older, and the way the world is, I don't know that I believe that anymore.

My 'friends' don't care about me, my family doesn't care, and I'm in a job that I don't like. I have no ambition and I don't see much of a future.

Dear reader,

You are not alone. Things and situations do happen. However, there is always a positive light for everything that is negative.

Continue to be that kind and helpful person that you are. It doesn't matter what people think of you. You are the one who can make a difference for yourself. Find things that you love or that you have been dreaming of doing. Chances are the job that you love is right within reach. Don't give up. Your friends and family will love you for just being you. That will never change.

Don't be afraid to have a sit down with your friends and family. Tell them how you feel. Don't keep your emotions bottled up. You'll feel better that you did. For jobs, there are so many options available. You may want to consider taking a course for something that may interest you. Believe or not, with online being so popular, you could find almost anything. Again, your goals are close. Keep striving!"

If you need advice, and don't know where to turn, reach out to us at pandemicpm@gmail.com. Please include the subject line" TLC Advice."

Thank you for your support. We invite you to follow and connect with our YouTube Channel, The CCI Radio Show. Please like, click, share and subscribe. You can also listen to our secondary shows, The CCI Radio Show "Gospel Excellence w/ The Angel of the Airwaves, Bobbie D" and The CCI Radio Show "Love Notes w/ Sam C Smooth" on Blogtalkradio, Soundcloud, Spotify, Anchor Podcasts and many other social media outlets. Our newest show, The CCI Radio Show "TLC Podcast" is also available on our YouTube Channel!

www.pandemicpresspublishing.com

Sam C On Sports

Welcome to the debut of Sam C On Sports! I will give you the latest sports news and info! Let's get started!

NFL Football: The NFL Draft happened at the end of April. There were a lot of surprises and developments. Of course, it wouldn't be the NFL Draft if there wasn't. One of the questions going into this draft were especially of interest to us Pittsburgh Steeler fans, since the retirement of Ben Roethlisberger. There will be big shoes to fill. Ben was the ultimate player of the game. The owners had their eyes on a few different college prospects. But, in the end, it was University of Pittsburgh Quarterback Kenny Pickett that was selected by the Steelers. At the time of this post, Training Camp is just around the corner. Many of the NFL teams will be opening up their stadiums/training sites to the fans for the first time since the start of the pandemic. That also means Preseason is coming soon. The NFL has dropped the number of Preseason games from 4 or 5 to 3. Will the LA Rams be able to win back to back Super Bowls? We shall see! This should be another great NFL Season!

Baseball: Major League Baseball was delayed once again. But, once it got rolling, there was no stopping it. America's pastime can now be seen on NBC on Sundays, along with streaming on Peacock. We are currently halfway through the season! The Atlanta Braves are fighting to win the World Series for a second year!

NBA: The NBA has reached the end of the regular season. The playoffs were brutal! At the end, we have a champion! The Golden State Warriors won it all! They overcome all of their issues and injuries! Congratulations!

WNBA: The WNBA has been full of nonstop action and thrills since the season started back! I'm excited to see the season start again! So far there have been some great games and rivalries. The Chicago Sky, the current champions, are set to defend their title! This should be another great season! However, our hearts and prayers go out to WNBA player Brittney Griner. At the time of this post, not only is she still captive in a Russian prison but she has pleaded guilty to drug charges as well. President Biden and his staff have contacted Griner's wife and are trying to find a way to step in and help.

USFL: The USFL has returned since its debut in the 80's! For all of us football lovers, it gives access to more football! The season came to an end recently with the Birmingham Stallions winning the championship. Congratulations on a great championship run!

NHL: Hockey has come and gone! It came down to the two time winner the Tampa Bay Lightning and the Colorado Avalanche! It was the Avalanche that upset the Lightning on their way to a Stanley Cup trophy! It's their first since 2001! Congratulations!

That's it for now! I'll have more next time!

The CUBB House Merch Store

Welcome to The CUBB House Merch Store! This month, we are featuring these following items! They are:

1. "Original Pandemic Press Media" short sleeve in Black and Gold
2. Pandemic Press Media Logo short sleeve in Gold
3. "New Logo" Pandemic Press Media short sleeve in Blue
4. Pandemic Press Publishing "New Logo" short sleeve in Sky Blue

For pricing information and If you would like to see the whole collection line, please visit https://www.pandemicpresspublishing.com/the-cubb-house-merch-store/ !

All items can be paid by CashApp (PandemicPressMedia) or PayPal (PandemicPressPublishing). Any questions, please contact pandemicpresspublishing@gmail.com!

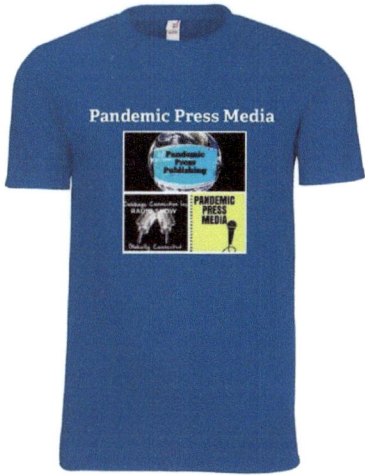

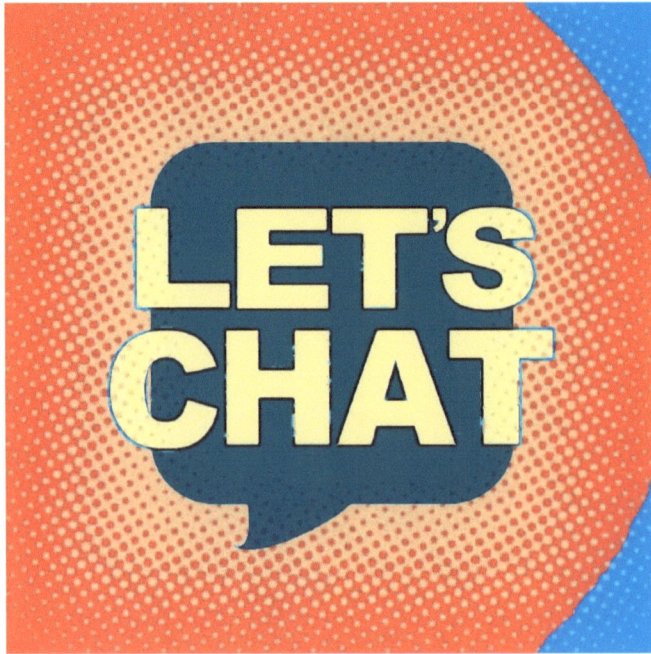

The CUBB House Chat

First: Did you know that The CCI Radio Show celebrated its 10th Anniversary this past January 1st? Yes! We initially started on the Blogtalkradio platform. The show has since branched off into 2 more versions. "Gospel Excellence w/ Bobbie D" is the home of 'The Best Gospel Music and Praise!', and "Love Notes" w/ Sam C Smooth is the home of 'all of your great Slow Jams and Love Songs'. It's "Music For Lovers!"

Each show is done on Sunday. Gospel Excellence is at 10AM EST and Love Notes is at 10PM EST on Blogtalkradio. The shows are also available on Soundcloud, Spotify and Anchor Podcasts soon after! Make sure to find us, especially on Spotify and Anchor Podcasts for any episodes that you may have missed! Currently, we are at Episode #583 on this platform…and climbing!!!

Spotify: https://open.spotify.com/show/0x519bbv8Ysy0OIQFkQpRj
Anchor Podcasts: https://anchor.fm/ccisbglobal
Soundcloud: https://soundcloud.com/ccisbglobal

Second: Did you know that The CCI Radio Show has also expanded to YouTube?! You can watch the show live Saturdays at 10AM EST! Recently, the show celebrated its 60th YouTube episode!

And you can't forget our NEW show, "The CCI TLC Radio Show Podcast"! This show focuses on what you want to do with your life's path. Do you want love, money, fame or fortune? Are you wondering how to achieve these goals? Do you want people to take you more seriously? Sam C. and Bobbie D. are certified Transitional Life Coaches, and are looking forward to helping you to find your way.

Also, "Cooking Fun w/ Mrs. Cubbage " has taken off! This cooking show, hosted by Bobbie Cubbage, is based off of her cookbook, of the same name, of course! The show is recorded and airs every Friday at 4PM EST on The CCI Radio Show YouTube Channel! Please make sure to like, click, share and subscribe to our channel! Hit the bell for all show notifications!

We look forward to more great things with our channel so stay tuned!!!

The CCI Radio Show YouTube Channel:
https://www.youtube.com/channel/UCd2hYN9wyUVRj-C0alaZc2Q

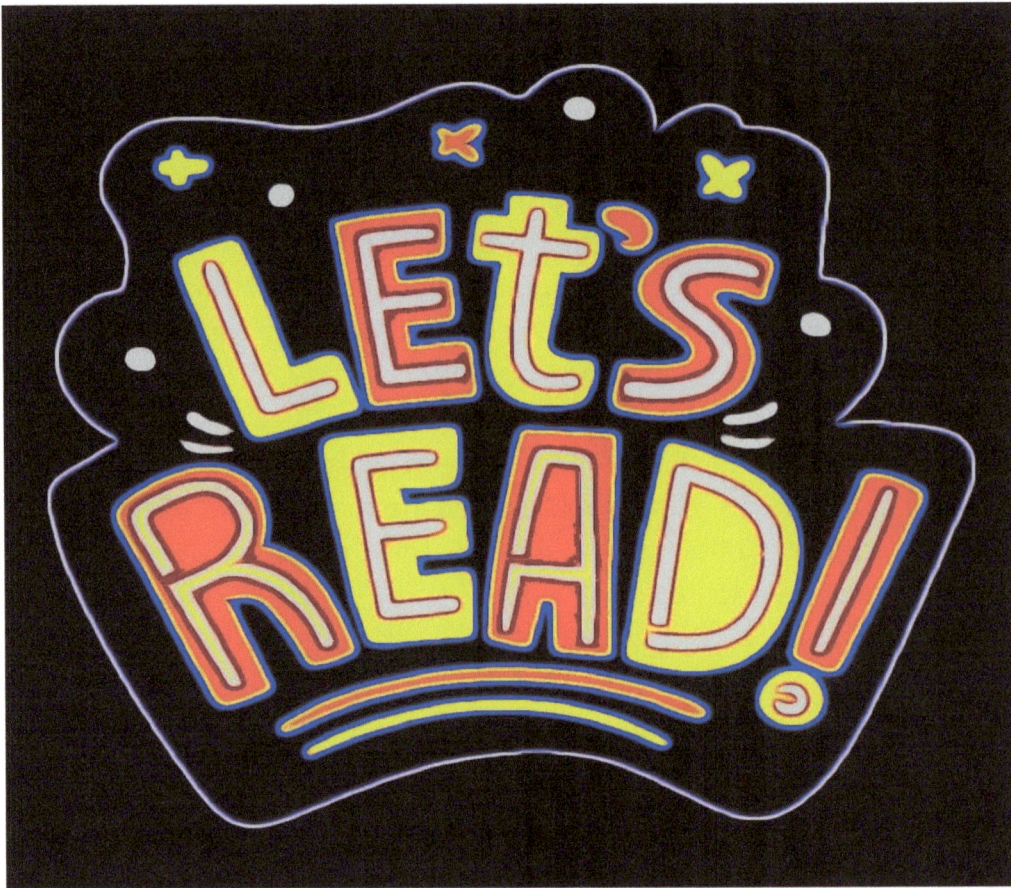

Here is a great book to add to your collection:

Cooking Fun w/ Mrs. Cubbage

"Cooking fun with Mrs. Cubbage", is a fun, lively, full-color cookbook, dedicated to all of the students that have been in Mrs. Cubbage's cooking classes over the years! Mrs. Cubbage is an Early Childhood educator, who works as a preschool teacher by day, and a community center after school teacher, in the afternoons. Tasty recipes, sprinkled with classroom stories, "Cooking Fun with Mrs. Cubbage" is SURE to delight the young; as well as the young at heart! Get your copy today at Lulu.com, Amazon.com and where books are sold!

Cooking Fun with Mrs. Cubbage

By Bobbie Cubbage

Pandemic Press Publishing

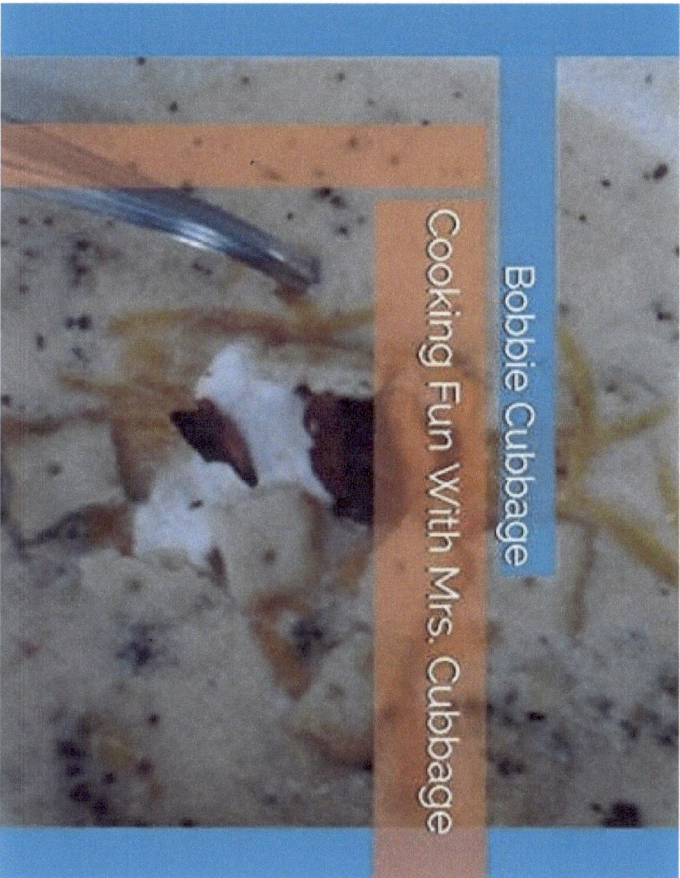

Bobbie Cubbage

Cooking Fun With Mrs. Cubbage

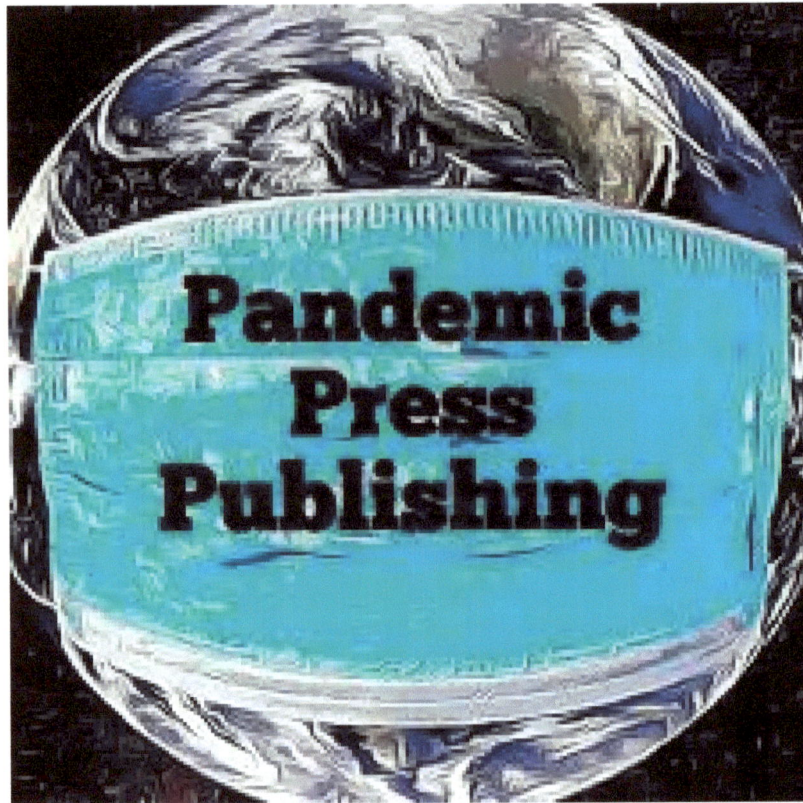

Looking to get your book or other item published? Well, look no further than Pandemic Press Publishing! We are Passionate about Writing, Passionate about Creativity! We are also more than just a publishing company! Contact us today for all of your needs at pandemicpp@gmail.com or visit www.pandemicpresspublishing.com!

Gospel Excellence w/ Bobbie D is one of the original shows which started out on Blogtalkradio. It is your home for the 'Best Gospel Music and Praise!" It's been on the air since 2012, and has since expanded to many other platforms, such as Anchor, Spotify, Soundcloud and more! You can catch Gospel Excellence every other Sunday on Blogtalkradio and where podcasts are available!

THE CCI RADIO SHOW

TLC

PODCAST

The newest edition to The CCI Radio Show programming schedule has arrived! It's The CCI Radio Show "TLC Podcast!" It will air every other Saturday morning at 10AM EST on our YouTube Channel, The CCI Radio Show. Certified Life Coaches, Sam C and Bobbie D will help to give some great and useful tips regarding relationships and more. We are excited and grateful to have you join us!

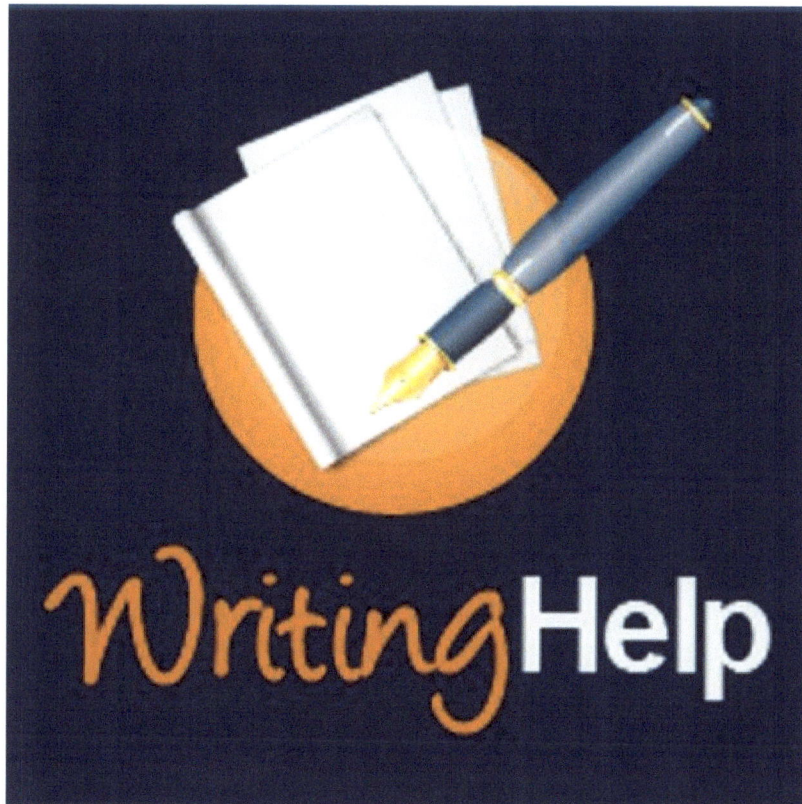

Are you looking for a little help, just to get some ideas for your writing? Look no further than Pandemic Press Publishing's "Writing Inspiration!" Our tips are very informative and worth a try! Lots of tips available! Visit https://www.pandemicpresspublishing.com/ppp-writing-inspiration/ right now!

Thank you

We want to take this time to say "Thank You" for reading this "Debut" edition of Pandemic Press Media Magazine! All of your kind words and your continued support is very much appreciated and does not go unnoticed! We look forward to bringing you more great content in our next edition. Stay Tuned!

SHARE IDEAS

Anything that you would like to see in our magazine? A certain recipe? Do you know someone who would like to be interviewed? Any interesting ideas at all? Let us know and we'll do our best to make it happen!